CHAMELEONS

JEANNE COWDEN

CHAMELEONS

The Little Lions of the Reptile World

With Photographs by the Author

DAVID McKAY COMPANY, INC. / NEW YORK

To my parents' grandchildren, in whose splendid young hands concern for our wildlife will continue in safekeeping, and to my sister "Pete," with my love and thanks.

COPYRIGHT © 1977 by Jeanne Cowden

Library of Congress Cataloging in Publication Data

Cowden, Jeanne.
    Chameleons: the little lions of the reptile world.

    SUMMARY: Describes the author's experiences with and observations of chameleons.
    1. Chameleons—Juvenile literature. [1.   Cha-
meleons]   I.   Title.
QL666.L23C68   598.1'12   76-16345
ISBN 0-679-20381-8

10 9 8 7 6 5 4 3 2 1

Manufactured in the United States of America

Contents

ONE
"Let Man Die"

"What did the poor chameleon do," I asked, "that he must be forever regarded as unlucky?"

The old Zulu did not answer immediately but looked searchingly at me, assessing his audience. With his three young sons and my four-year-old nephew, we sat on the great trunk of a giant milkwood tree that had crashed to the ground during a storm. In this way, I thought, from father to son, the legends and folklore of Africa have been handed down.

"You must understand,' he began, "that it was what the chameleon did *not* do." He let this statement sink in, then went on. "Umwabe [the chameleon] was called to Un-kulunkulu [the Creator] and entrusted with an important mission, but because he was as he was, and is, he it was who lost for Man the hope of life after death."

I thought this a heavy burden for such a small creature to bear, and something of this must have shown on my face, the old Zulu flashed a sudden smile of understanding, dazzling white against a luxurious black beard. "You are Nkosazane uthanda izilwane zasehlathini—the girl who loves animals and the forest—and therefore you are drawn to Umwabe; perhaps specially to him as there is no living thing like him. He came from before time and has remained that way. He is different. And perhaps this is the reason the Unkulunkulu chose him and left him as he is."

I said nothing. It is discourteous, indeed almost impossible, to hurry conversation with a Zulu, who has a long background where time has meant little. Each sentence uttered is given time for the mental picture to be formed and understood. In my mind's eye I conjured up the patient chameleon responding, in its characteristic, deliberate way, to the Creator's summons.

"Let me tell you how it was," the old man continued, satisfied that my mind was receptive to what was to follow. "And Unkulunkulu said: 'Let Man not die. This is my message.' Umwabe waited patiently for his instructions, since the words did not seem to him to have any sense of direction. 'Go,' commanded Unkulunkulu. 'Go and find Man and deliver my word to him: Let Man not die.'

"And Umwabe set off. He was a slow creature, as you know, both in walking and in finding food to sustain him on the way. So slow that Unkulunkulu sent a second messenger. This time it was the blue-headed lizard, and being quick in movement, he found Man and announced *his* message: 'Let Man die.' "

The narrator forestalled my obvious intention to interrupt. "Who is to say when Unkulunkulu changed His mind?" he supplied in reply to my unvoiced question. "Some even say that He sent both at the same time and that the lizard found Man first. But it followed that Man accepted the first word of Unkulunkulu: 'Let Man die'; and when Umwabe eventually arrived with his given words, 'Let Man not die,' Man said, 'But we have already heard the word of Unkulunkulu and our ears are deaf to any other. Had you come first, we should have believed you. Now you are too late.' "

The old man nodded permission for me to speak, and I

immediately took up cudgels on the chameleon's behalf. "There is one story," I remarked, "that it was not Umwabe's fault at all, that the inquisitive, mischievous lizard by chance overheard the confidential words between Umwabe and Unkulunkulu and, from pure devilry and without thought, bounded off and handed on the contrary word to Man."

He benignly agreed. "There are many versions, but the result is the same. It was not thought that Man could escape death, but Umwabe was entrusted with an important mission, and in failing to execute it, for whatever reason, it is his fault entirely that Man could not return to life after death."

From the tree trunk where we sat, we had been quietly watching a small bushbuck in the undergrowth. The old man's whispered story about it had been interrupted when I had noticed the chameleon making its way toward us and asked the origin of its aura of misfortune. The Zulu boys drew away from it, but their imperturbable father knew that it had a considerable distance to cover and would do it slowly. He had time enough to tell his story.

The chameleon laboring over the uneven surface jerked drunkenly. Bare of a tail, it looked like a tightrope walker minus a balancing pole, or a jet with its high rear structure missing. It was a female of the Flap-neck variety, about fifteen centimeters long without its tail; where that had been was a gory stump. The injury had probably been caused unwittingly by cane cutters, although knowing the profound superstition surrounding a chameleon, I reserved judgment on this.

A Zulu will not touch a chameleon, nor does he like to see anyone else do so, but the old storyteller and his family showed an understanding tolerance for me—this friend who loved the bush. From then on, if they came across chameleons, someone was immediately sent to tell me.

Soon I was left alone, watching the maimed female approach me. She was terrified of making each move and, after a few steps, crouched motionless as if trying to regain the balance disturbed by the loss of her tail.

Her kind was forever condemned by legend. But not by

me. And my message was "Let her not die." So I took her home and there, in the tropical climate beloved by chameleons, she found peace and health, choosing a fever tree with long, white lethal thorns, which protected her from predators, mainly large wild birds that dropped down, from time to time, to share my garden.

The loss of her tail, besides affecting her balance, also limited her hunting. She lacked the precision of synchronized tongue and eyes, and she often lost her balance at the moment of her tongue's impact on an insect. She became quite content, after a while, to rely on me to supplement the food supply in the vicinity of her chosen tree, and so endeared herself to the family, as many of her kind do to South Africans.

The tail did not grow again. When the wound healed, she completely shed her skin and, with the revelation of the new one, regained health and assurance. But having found that this particular tree guaranteed safety and food, she seldom ventured away and always returned to the same branch to sleep. During the three years that followed, she sometimes disappeared during the winter months of June through August but reappeared in the spring.

The fourth year I saw the familiar outline and welcomed her. Some time later she disappeared, and all the signs and investigations pointed to someone having taken her from the garden.

I missed her a great deal. But she left something of herself with me. That tailless Flap-neck sowed in me the seed that, comfortably dormant then, would grow in interest and fascination.

TWO
Chameleon, Human and Legend Weave a Tapestry

I have lived in tropical Natal for most of my life, and the tailless Flap-neck brought back remembrances of my childhood, when life's tempo seemed slower and less anxious, and when chameleons were so prevalent that it was common to see them sunning themselves on wire fences or making their laborious way from one side of the road to the other. Often I took one home to a bush in the garden and delighted in the ease with which it became part of the family, waiting for the gifts of insect food, which it took with a lightning flick of a projected tongue.

I knew that like the cycad, one of which grows in my garden, the chameleon has survived through millions of years; that it had some unique features; that the Zulus abhor it; and that the larger green species lays its eggs in the ground. But what of its life cycle?

"He that increaseth knowledge increaseth sorrow," I remembered. But I decided now to disregard the warning in Ecclesiastes and to set about finding answers to the chameleon's missing links. Books seemed to add little real light, only a little confusion.

There was nothing to do but find out at firsthand.

As is often the case, when one has a casual interest in something in Nature, it is much in evidence; but when the interest becomes important, that something perversely disappears. So it was with chameleons. The growing pattern in the wild is for its inhabitants to put as much distance as possible between man, the universal destroyer, and themselves. Chameleons, it seemed, had joined the great retreat. They did not appear as often any more. Apart from this, it seems to me that some years are "chameleon years," others not.

About a kilometer from where I live and barely twenty kilometers from the city of Durban is a small indigenous forest. On one side of it is the Umhlanga River; on another, sugar cane fields. At one time, the forest swept down in unbroken wilderness to the edge of the lagoon created by the Umhlanga before it joins the Indian Ocean. The lagoon formed the third side of a rough triangle. Some years ago, a freeway was cut through the trees just above the lagoon, and a wedge of swamp was left between the road, still lined with thick bush, and the high sand dunes topped with dense undergrowth, giant trees and tall aloes.

Umhlanga is the Zulu word for "river of reeds"; and the trapped swamp, undisturbed and sheltered, brought the words to vigorous reality. White silky plumes waved and the movement of water and breeze jostled the tall reeds. Where the water reluctantly gave way to more solid earth there had been, many years ago, neat paddy fields wrung and molded from the swamp. The water was then channeled to the rice plants and lusty banana trees, which lounged about in haphazard clumps. It was a paradise for wild birds and monkeys ever on the hunt for handouts of grain and fruit.

But when Nature triumphs over man, it is with inexorable efficiency. Lush vegetation and rampant vines, thriving alongside the rice, waited for the opportunity to creep in, overpower and choke it, and clothe the man-made nakedness of the earth. Even man, the original ravisher of the land, finally gave up the struggle against the rapacious tenacity of a swamp wanting to reclaim its own. Bushes and saplings took root. With the disappearance of the rice, the small grain-eating birds were replaced with larger species, more in keeping with the generous growth all around. Frogs had always been constant voices in the many-octaved music that always accompanied the untamed beauty of this Little Bush.

The score was rewritten. The high-key melody of finches, warblers and weavers that had been heard with the frogs was missing. Now there was the distinctive solo of the fish eagle, the clear question posed and answer given by the louries, the sonorous boom of bitterns and the full-throated cry of wild geese echoing across the marsh. Water birds returned; pythons moved about in the dense swampy terrain, which was rife with dragonflies, butterflies and grasshoppers. It became a small, safe place for the wild. And one of my favorite places.

Just as beloved and overgrown, but in a different way, is my large garden, which runs to the sea in a confusion of trees and flowers through a last bastion of rare giant aloe thraskii and beach bush. Discovered by my parents over twenty-five years ago, the old house and garden, doomed and vulnerable, are anachronisms in the encroaching concrete. The Little Bush and my garden—already a haven for countless wild birds—became sanctuaries for chameleons saved from traffic, tormented by fearful cane cutters, or threatened in any way. Friends and family, amusedly tolerant as always of my wildlife exploits, now no longer only felt a pang of pity, nor were they at a loss to know what to do with an unfortunate chameleon; they were relieved to bring it to me. Over the years the number grew—both in my garden and in the bush—and although a few ventured away, there were always chameleons around me.

Once I found a shoe box that had been left on my veranda. Across the lid was a hastily scrawled message: "One damned vicious brontosaurus within! Gave me a hard time on the highway." Another time, a telephone call: "Did you find one of your monsters in the garden? I caused a traffic jam as I leaped from my truck to save it from the wheels of a bus." I went out to the described bush and found it, calmly lazing in the sun, oblivious of the disturbance it had created.

The only people I encountered in my small wilderness were Zulus and, to a lesser extent, Indian children. I often had the company of little Zulu boys who, although detesting chameleons, liked to be with me and took great delight in vying with each other to "find" chameleons for me, although they most often turned out to be the ones I knew already. Sometimes, although they recognized those identified by scars, shortened tails or distinctive marks, as I did, they pointed them out as a discovery, unable to resist the temptation to earn my thanks. Not even for me, though, would they go near them or touch them.

"One of your animals and I have looked at each other," a boy would report. Zulu lore provides heaven shepherds, who herd the clouds, just as the small boys on earth, at an early age, are "herd boys" for the family's cattle. I called my small friends Imelus Umwabe—herd boys of the chameleons—and, if a little dubious about its association, they still beamed at the pleasurable status of a title.

Chameleons are diurnal. Past masters in the art of camouflage, they spend most of their time in trees, descending to the ground only when it is necessary to find food and, in some species, to lay their eggs. During the hours of darkness when they sleep, their skin assumes a pale luminous color, easily highlighted in the beam of a flashlight. In this way I could pinpoint them at night and knew where to find them the following day. I discovered them often to be creatures of habit and found that they stayed in the same area, and even slept in the same tree, when the food supply and environment were to their liking. In this way they are part of our country scene; and here in South Africa, people often say: "Meet our Chameleon. It has been with us for years."

I had only the time before and after office hours, and weekends, during which to be in the forest and my garden. Fortunately, chameleons are active and around during the summer months, when the hours of daylight afforded me more time to watch them. But at this stage they did not claim all my attention, as they shared my interest with countless other facets of the wild. Nevertheless, although I was not yet completely engrossed, I did, indeed, "increaseth knowledge" about the two species in my area—the large green egg-laying Flap-neck *Chamaeleo dilepis;* and later, the live-bearing pygmy *Microsaura pumila.*

Could the discomfort in the rain, the lonely watching, the frustration of not having enough time and the increasing knowledge be defined as those things that "increaseth sorrow?" In a way, yes. There was a sadness in me for the harsh context of this small creature's life, the enormity of the hazards that threaten it and how ill-equipped it is to perform the things demanded of it.

I became involved in its world and knew a sense of futility in not being able to intervene or to lighten the burden of Nature's harsh and rigid laws. And, inevitably, I became attached to those who responded to my gesture of friendship. They all may have looked similar on the surface, but there were marked differences in their chameleon "personalities."

Close association always uncovers individuality. I got to know them. And, after the winter months, when most of them disappeared into semi-hibernation, it was a joy to recognize those I knew and give a grin of welcome to a known green form lying along a sun-drenched branch, or feel disappointment when a favorite did not reappear. For how is it possible to know a creature of the wild, earn its trust and not feel affection, concern and a sort of responsibility for its safety?

With dignity and patience, unaggressive wild creatures accept intrusion, even man, if the approach is clearly one of peace, if movements are calm and consistent. Abrupt clumsiness instantly destroys any hope of rapport. The whole outline in the creature's vision is assessed by communication of senses. The outline either threatens or it does not. And in my garden, and the Little Bush, it was not difficult to find the tranquillity our friendship needed.

Often it takes a chance moment, a fleeting glance, an unexpected encounter, to change aimless wondering into definite action. My little tailless chameleon was the spark to the idle curiosity I had always had about chameleons. But it was a large, green female Flap-neck *Chamaeleo dilepis* and a smaller male that, in the hour of a tropical dawn, took possession of my mind and imagination and, for the next five years, all my leisure hours.

THREE
The Golden Catalysts

It was the last day of January—a genesis of a morning when "the earth was without form, and void; and darkness was upon the face of the deep."

I leaned against an age-old milkwood tree, as I often do, to watch a tree spangled with sleeping white egrets transformed by the sun into glowing candles and to see the birds shimmer into graceful flight.

I could sense life beginning to teem around me, undefined in the still misty light but like a steady subterranean disturbance, bubbling to the surface in the swish of small wings, the scuttling of leaves, the plop of small bodies hitting water. The haunting cry of the coucal, legendary harbinger of rain, soon gave way to the duet of boubou shrikes sharing their love.

Before me stood an old tree, burned by lightning to a skeletal gray. As the sun poured over it, something moved.

A small grotesque form on an outflung branch reared,

gleaming like rippling gold. And through the vapor rising from the earth, a small replica moved toward the bole of the tree. It hesitated because of the obvious menace from above, then continued its determined, upward way.

I was observing a pair of chameleons.

Time in the wild has little meaning, since it flows in a never ending tide, and there is scant need to harness or discipline it unless instinct or the urgency of the seasons requests it.

Now it was measured by the ritual of the chameleons' mating move and countermove, in patient wooing, watchfulness, encouragement and rejection, which erupted into brief violence, subsided, then erupted again, while the nuptial ceremony ran its course.

"The Lightning Bird did it. It came from heaven country and tried to kill them" explained one of my young Zulu friends.

Quietly, I explained that the tree had, as they could well see, received its mortal wound a long time before the chameleons just happened to be there. They solemnly shook their heads. To a Zulu, lightning comes in a living shape, most often that of a bird. In some tribes, so close is this tie-up that the fish eagle and the "bird of heaven" have the same name. The bird flies in the clouds, and when it drops down like a thunderbolt to exact punishment, it is too fast for the human eye, which can only register a flash as the bird passes and strikes. Where it hits the ground, it lays a large egg. Others believe that when the enormous bird in heaven country prepares to come to earth, it ruffles its feathers; the lightning is the sheen, and the subsequent crash of thunder is the rush of its giant wings as it surges down to earth.

So apprehensive is a Zulu of a tree that has been struck by lightning that he will not use it for firewood.

My dawn chameleon pair had made an unfortunate choice, and already unpopular, they were now a further target of superstition. The two small watchers with me crept away, leaving me alone to absorb the drama unfolding before me.

The poetic quality of the dawn passed into the hard, bright glare of mid-morning, and the two small silhouettes were noosed together against the burning sun. Even in this light the mystique of the day's creation lingered, giving them the illusion of a lost age.

The quiet culmination of their mating was strangely at variance with the initial ferocity. The male eventually moved away, out of his mate's life, and disappeared into a clump of trees. He would know nothing of the birth of his offspring. He had no parental ties whatsoever, nor would the female, after the laying of her eggs.

She lay in the sun, solitary, abandoned, awaiting the destined cycle, to play her part in bearing the next generation. Even she, a lesser being not credited with emotion, surely had the special, serene look of expectant motherhood.

FOUR
Portrait of a Little Lion

There is an old French proverb: "Afrique est coutumière toujours choses produire nouvelles et monstrueuses." It is the custom of Africa to produce new and monstrous things.

Africa is the natural habitat of chameleons. Half of them, except for a few species in India and in the vicinity of the Mediterranean, come from Africa south of the Sahara. The other half come from Madagascar, the large island off the East African coast.

New? The chameleon cannot lay claim to that, but its singular appearance, unchanged for millions of years, will always evoke fresh interest. Monstrous? How could it not be when it evolved from an entirely Old World family of lizards—the agamids—and has survived from the time of prehistory?

The Greeks, who were responsible for the descriptive names of the dinosaurs, also gave the chameleon its name: *khami*—on the ground—and *leon*—lion. It was known to them as "little lion," and they were fascinated by its courage when threatened or tormented, and by the way it blew itself up, hissed and waved its tail in anger—a tiny, strange creature but with all the pride and aggression of the king of the beasts.

Today, chameleons belong to the family Chamaeleonidae and genus *Chamaeleo*. They are grouped with the lizard section of reptiles. There are eighty species of chameleons. One of the largest comes from East Africa—*Chamaeleo melleri*—and is about two feet in length. *Chamaeleo fischeri*, from the same area, has two horns protruding from its snout; *Chamealeo oweni*, from the Congo, has three such bony outgrowths. The South African *Chamaeleo namaquensis* has a comparatively shorter tail. The most common species in South Africa, and especially in Natal, is the oviparous Flapneck, *Chamaeleo dilepis*. This species and the dwarf, viviparous *Microsaura pumila* are the two in which I observed the full life cycle.

I began to study each unique part that made up the antediluvian, bizarre whole of the little lion.

Alfonso, King of Castile, called "The Wise," once said: "If I had been present at the Creation, I would have given some useful hints for the better arrangement of the Universe." And the more I found out about the chameleon, the greater was my feeling that the chameleon had, indeed, plodded awkwardly down the ages, overlooked in adaptations, mutations and evolutions. I agreed with the King of Castile: The chameleon would be the first in line for some improvements, some adaptations of features that may have been feasible when the world was a vastly different place but that had not kept up with environmental changes. Each time I looked at a chameleon I marveled how one small living thing could survive, unchanged, for so long.

Many lizards, especially with the capacity to change color and project their tongues, are erroneously labeled chameleons. Lizards are darting reptiles with tails that are unable to grasp but can grow again when damaged; chameleons are slow-moving creatures with prehensile tails that, once damaged, are not replaced. The true chameleon also has unique characteristics with respect to its eyes, tongue and the composition of its toes.

The large green oviparous Flap-neck is typical Chamaeleonidae. The full grown female is larger than the male. She averages fifteen to twenty centimeters from snout to tail-tip, while the male is about twelve to fifteen centimeters long. They look very similar during the first year, but into the second year, the female broadens while the male remains lean and wiry. There are variations of color and markings as well. Normally, the male is green or green-brown; the female is brighter, and of those in my vicinity, some have a white slash along the side of the body, others are mottled dark and light green, and others are plain yellow-green.

One of the chameleon's greatest claims to fame is its ability to change color. This is a protective device of camouflage in its natural environment—trees. However, changing its color is also governed by temperature, emotion and light. If one side of the body is in the sun and the other in shadow, the former is darker than the latter; if part of its sunbathed body is obscured by a leaf or twig, there will be a large expanse of dark green, with the paler outline of a leaf clearly defined. They love warmth, and often, as they bask in the fierce heat of the African sun, they become almost black. Black is also the color they affect when angry or afraid; and the male often becomes dark with tense anxiety when trying to win a mate.

The female has her own distinctive mating color scheme. Her skin turns a darker shade of green, and it becomes covered with small yellowish spots. This was, to me, always a giveaway. In the mating season, even if a male was invisible, the female sensed his presence, and I knew by her spots that there was a male nearby.

When she is preparing to lay her eggs, the female changes her noticeable clear light-green hue to a deeper greenish black, quite often mottled. I put this down either to a protective measure to merge in with the dark earth and grass, or from sensitive strain and anxiety. Or, perhaps, both.

A chameleon's head is blunt and bony, and elongates into

a flap over the neck, giving the whole face a resemblance to a mask or helmet. The spine is like a ridge rising from under the flap and from which, on either side, the skin—minutely scaly, granulated, and cold and clammy to the touch—falls away so that the body, almost flat from spine to belly, looks as though it is standing on edge. Thus vertically flattened, it serves a dual purpose. From above, when the chameleon is in repose, the spine can be easily mistaken for the edge of another leaf; and this illusion is furthered as, swaying slowly, the chameleon simulates to perfection a gently waving leaf. Confronted by an enemy, it turns its flattened body sideways, draws itself up and succeeds in looking twice its size. Add to this a throat that blows up to reveal vivid yellow-orange stripes and a whole attitude grotesque in menace, and the sum total is one of vivid, if illusory, warning. A chameleon does not seek confrontation, as it has little with which to do battle; but if it is attacked or threatened, it gives a good account of itself as it hisses, snaps, rears its darkened body, lunges at its adversary and, ounce for ounce, represents a far more formidable threat than some predators twice its size.

"I am sure," one of my small Zulu companions offered, "that Unkulunkulu chose Umwabe to take the one great message because of his only eyes."

"Only eyes?"

"Yes, only he has them. One can see in front, one can see behind, both at the same time. Everywhere eyes." He drew closer to me and confided, "that is why I do not like Umwabe. He is like an evil spirit that can see right into you. Wherever I am, one of his eyes follows me."

I could think of little that was less evil than the peaceable chameleon we were watching. It asked nothing other than to find a few insects, enjoy the sun and be left alone. But, as the small boy left me, one eye of the chameleon watched his departure while the other was on me. A plane flew overhead, and it kept this in view with the eye that had followed the boy out of sight. This capacity to pick up the movements of birds and aircraft high in the sky never fails to amaze me, especially as the chameleon follows the objects until they disappear, even if only with one eye.

The eyelids are fused into spherical, bulging protuberances situated on either side of the head. In the center of each is a tiny opening like the stopped-down aperture of a camera lens. Deep inside this can be seen the brightly shining eye itself. In most females I saw, the color was amber, while it was almost red in the males. The eye turrets have the disconcerting capacity to swivel in any direction independently of each other, like the guns on a tank. The whole chameleon, in fact, has the appearance of a miniature, slow-moving tank. The eye phenomenon allows two complete fields of vision with an equally sharp image in each. Immediately as one of the roving turrets fixes on prey or danger, the other swings to the same point of focus. The result of this synchronization is a binocular effect that gives a detailed picture of crystal clarity. This perfect vision is adversely affected if the partnership breaks down. Chameleons that suffer injury to one eye appear confused and lack confidence and balance. But, more seriously, the vital aim of the tongue is impaired.

I came across a theory that chameleons do not see in color. However, I noticed that they do not eat the highly colored grasshoppers, commonly known as "stinkers," or "soldiers," even though they are fat and soft; and, in general, avoid butterflies and insects with the "warning colors" of Nature. This could, of course, be because of a repelling smell or taste.

Tongue and eyes are a powerful combination for judgment in distance and accuracy. A chameleon cannot spring on its prey to deal with it at close quarters. Slow moving, it relies on the dexterity of its tongue to project at lightning speed and trap its insect food on a sticky tip. The tongue then shoots back into its mouth with the prey.

My early general impression was that the tongue lay rolled up in the chameleon's mouth, unraveled to flick at the insect, then rolled back into the mouth, very much like those "party novelties" in the shape of a narrow flat piece of paper that, blown out into a tube to its full length, curls back toward the mouthpiece when the air escapes. It is, however, much more complex and is wondrously fashioned.

It lies in the mouth like a tubular piece of elastic, bunched, concertinalike, toward the throat. Imagine that the chameleon has focused both eyes on an insect and moves its head forward in position to aim its tongue. It opens its mouth. Powerful muscles, which start in the throat and continue along the bottom jaw, move the whole tongue forward; the same muscles will pull the tongue back. The concertinalike crinkles at the back, which tuck the long tongue into the mouth when not in use, are muscles that, when extended, give the tongue its length. The end of the tongue is made up of a tendon elongated from the concertina muscles. It is a hollow tube inside which runs a gristlelike spike, lubricated by mucus.

The tongue is ready for action. But what propels it?

Above the point where the concertina muscles become the thin tendon lie other powerful muscles that give the tongue its acceleration. The whole tongue tip, therefore, is made up of accelerator muscles on either side of the tendon that carries the bony spike.

With this marvelous, unique combination, the chameleon is ready for the finale. At the moment of "shooting the tongue," the accelerator muscles pull the entire bell-tip off the spike, turning the tendon inside out so that spike, tendon and accelerator muscles are one long line making straight for the prey, with a reach longer than the chameleon itself. The tip that strikes the prey is like a club, or bell, hollowed out at the end and covered in sticky fluid. There is a distinct moment of suction as the shallow walls wrap around, or extend over, the insect. Adhesion is powerful, and sometimes a chameleon strikes a large grasshopper that clings strongly to grass or twig. The chameleon's tongue grip is equally strong. Instead of letting go, its whole body scrambles after its tongue, as though the positions were reversed, and the body retracts to tongue and insect's anchor. There are no teeth but vicelike serrated jaws close over the hapless grasshopper, and it is torn remorselessly from its hold.

Chameleons eat voraciously when food is plentiful, but judging from the extreme thinness of some, I found (outside the semi-hibernation period) that they can exist for long periods without food. Once, near a group of houses in the cane fields where I had not been for some time, the children took me to a dead tree. On a branch was a large female chameleon. I suspect that, tormented, she was terrified to leave, and my fears were borne out. "It's been there since Christmas," they told me, "and we won't let it go away. It's going to stay there." Four weeks! I was appalled.

Her body was light. She was all bony head and hanging skin. I took her home, and her immediate problem was one of dehydration.

A chameleon does not lap water. From leaves drenched with rain or dew it takes moisture by pressing the tip of its tongue against the wet surface.

I spattered the bushes with water, and she absorbed it gratefully. That first day she was incapable of having enough and crawled from leaf to leaf ensuring, too, that her body brushed against the dampness around her. The next day, with her tongue lubricated and with that valiant tenacity special to the wild, she was game to try and eat. Easily recognizable by a black line scored across her snout, she lay in the garden and has been in and out of my life for over three years.

One way in which a chameleon attempts to provide a certain supply of food is to position its droppings on leaves. This attracts flies that are then only a tongue-length away.

As if my little lion does not have enough to make it noteworthy, its feet are peculiar to its own kind and are not found on any other member of the entire reptile family. A chameleon has strong hind legs, and it can hang down to get closer to its prey, then effortlessly draw itself up again to the branch. Hands and feet have two segments, or fingers, protruding from the wrists. On the end of these are short, sharp, separated claws. And this is where the uniqueness comes in: The hands have two claws on the outer finger and three on the inner, whereas the feet have the reverse arrangement—three on the outer segment, two on the inner.

It is difficult not to refer to "hands," since a chameleon uses its forelegs like hands. This opposite grouping of claws results in a remarkably powerful grip. A tiny body locked to a branch being whipped in all directions by a tree-flattening gale is a breathtaking sight, yet an inspiring one, knowing the tenacity of those toes.

The capacity to change skin is a prevalent one in the reptile family, and the chameleon is no exception. During the hot summer months especially, chameleons shed their skins quite regularly. I noticed, too, that, if the chameleon is angry or afraid to a degree of high tension, within a short time the skin invariably starts to peel off. The tailless chameleon's injury seemed to demand a skin change. After laying, as well, the females quite often deem it necessary to have a new skin. The first sign is usually a whitish bloom the outer skin assumes as it gently leaves the body but still protectively encases the new skin beneath until it is tough enough to withstand the elements. Then the outer skin starts to fray, more often than not at the elbow crease, where a split appears, and this is followed by skin cracks all over the body. The eye turrets revolve flimsy scales, and the tail waves flags of white as the shedding gains momentum. In some the process is quick and easy, as whole sheets drop off; in others, the skin clings and the chameleon rubs its body against the bark of a tree or scratches at its eyes and mouth with its hands or feet. But, within two days, there is not a vestige of the old covering left, and the chameleon looks out on the world in pristine newness.

There it hangs against the wall of today's wild, the portrait of a being out of time. The stark beauty of a brilliantly sculpted head; the cold-blooded body that houses unique eyes, tongue, toes and prehensile tail . . . all captured in the likeness of an agamid called chameleon.

FIVE
Midwife to a Chameleon

"Why does laughter come from your inside, Nkosa-zane?" my small friend asked.

Why, indeed? Because I knew my chameleon, heavy with eggs, was swaying on a wind-clutched branch somewhere in the murk and because, knowing I was going to have time on my hands while I waited to find her, I had drifted into some silly daydreaming.

"I smile," I offered, thinking to make him laugh, "because I think of Umwabe so much that I begin to be like her." Oh, no, I thought, that is not at all what I mean, so I tried again. "I was wondering if I could be as good a tree climber."

He looked at me gravely. "I do not share your smile, for I am glad you are not in the shape of Umwabe. But I smile when I tell you that you are quicker at reaching the top of the tree, and you at least throw the fruit down to us when you get there."

I do not, as a rule, give members of the wild human names. But because the female chameleons were outwardly so much alike, except for distinctive marks, and because I became unabashedly attached to those I got to know, I found myself mentally referring to the one with two scratches as Samantha, the one with a shortened tail as Dinny, yet another with a missing toe as Abigail and so on. The first pair that had earned my devotion became Pro, for the male, and Topsy, for the female. Pro, understandably, was not long in going about his business, and I only caught spasmodic glimpses of him. Topsy was with me for years.

It had rained all night, and the bush was still veiled in its aftermath. Leaves reflected the glint of sun where it shone through; otherwise, visibility was limited to about three meters. When the sun vanquished the remnants of the rain, I could feel that a summer haze would take over. While I waited to see Topsy, I was beguiled by the kaleidoscopic fragments in orbit and at my feet.

A dragonfly cruised past, to return and fling me a glance with its incredible compounded eyes of 30,000 units. At the slightest movement, it darted away, the fastest of all insects, capable of a speed of 60 miles per hour. Its lovely gauze wings and slender blue body gave an appearance of fragile nobility until, with savage decision, it took possession of a mate by grabbing her head and making her a prisoner.

I am always dumbfounded by the complexity and pas- sionate detail in Nature's methods of propagation. I should have thought it better for the danger-fraught process in such small living things to be brief and swift—for maturity to come soon, especially in view of the odds against their ever reaching it. Yet the elegant dragonfly has a comparatively long life in a completely different form before it turns into the ultimate flying beauty. The creature that emerges from the eggs, laid in water, is a nymph, wingless and brown. It eats and grows. And each time it becomes too large for its skeleton case, it cracks and the nymph appears with a soft shell. Wings, absent in the beginning, start to show and grow longer with each molt. It seems a long, laborious way of producing dragonflies.

On either side of my feet the earth displayed its own small denizens. Nature was full of industry, flamboyant in the clammy warmth—weaving webs, setting traps, digging tun- nels in preparation for the slenderest hope of survival. An antlion, tiny larva of a flying insect similar to the dragonfly, constructed a small, conical pit, maneuvered itself into the bottom so that only a pair of pincer-jaws protruded and waited for its breakfast. It came in the form of an unsuspecting ant. This was one time, I thought wryly, where "go to the ant, thou sluggard; consider her ways, and be wise" does not come off. This ant's curiosity, as it looked over the rim, got the better of its wisdom. It toppled into the pit and into the waiting perforated jaws that would suck its body dry of juices.

The rain had induced "flying ants" into the open, and these winged termites were erupting from holes in the damp earth. Males and females jostled in desperate effort to squeeze through the small openings that would take them to the next part of their metamorphosis, and to freedom. Blind soldiers packed around the holes, waving huge jaws to intimidate would-be attackers. And there was an increasing array of contenders for the steady stream of ant mass pouring out.

The flying ants fluttered flimsy wings and attempted to get airborne for the mating flight. More often than not, they collapsed in clumsy confusion, and when there were no more soldiers to watch over them, they were immediately snapped up by birds, frogs and lizards. Those that managed to crawl away and escape the onslaught shed their wings and, remarkably, managed to pair off to found their own dynasty somewhere in the vast expanse of earth.

In the midst of this drama, I caught sight of a little lumbering chameleon, making its way from a tree to the fount of food provided by the flying ants. She crouched amongst the other predators, helping to demoralize the soldiers, her tongue in perpetual motion, eating her fill.

Topsy lost her prehistoric dignity in abandoned greediness, as had the other creatures surrounding this unexpected horn of plenty, and a warm sense of gladness pervaded me that, on this morning at least, they would all know an unaccustomed satiation.

I studied her as she added food to her already overweight body. No reference could enlighten me on the gestation period. It was now a month since she had mated.

I have since watched the egg laying process many times.

As the weeks after mating pass, the female becomes heavier and more clumsy, and toward the end, she moves about as little as possible. The eggs inside seem to take up the whole of her body, which perhaps accounts for her comparative lack of interest in food. If disturbed when she first descends to start digging, she returns to the trees, sometimes for many days. I would become alarmed when this happened, as the shape of the eggs could clearly be seen bulging through the skin, bursting to be laid. For this reason the gestation period varies. It is anywhere between four and seven weeks. One pair mated on February 2 and the female laid on March 8, just over four weeks later. Yet another took six weeks; another, seven weeks.

One female I kept under observation in my garden surprised me by laying twenty eggs, although I was convinced she had not mated. I was told of a theory that it is not impossible for females to retain sperm in their bodies from a previous mating in case a male does not appear at the once-a-year, critically short time when a female can mate.

Topsy would need little food during the next few days, so she would not move far afield. But I wanted to be present when she laid, and I did not know what particular site she would choose. I contemplated taking her home so that she would lay in my garden but decided against it.

Early one morning, two weeks later and almost six weeks since she had mated, she was down on the ground, tail waving, looking about her; but after a while, she went back up the tree. Although the shape of the eggs showed through her skin, it was not yet time. She was obviously near laying and I was disappointed that, being Friday, I could not stay with her. My small Zulu friend agreed, reluctantly, to watch where she dug the hole. I would have to be content with that.

I was no sooner home and unhappily preparing to go to the office when my watcher catapulted into the house. "Your Umwabe," he panted. "You must come. I-Tekwane has it." We rushed back.

A hammerhead bird nonchantly tossed Topsy into the air, waited for her to fall and flounder, then threw her up again. Furiously plucky, sides heaving, jaws hissing, she defied the large bird but was no match for it in size or strength. But I was. And I used my superiority on her behalf. The small boy was dubious. I-Tekwane was full of dire connotations with lightning. To upset it or destroy its nest was to bring down anger in the form of violent rain. And, of course, there was Umwabe to add to this threat. He watched the triangular spectacle with neutral apprehension.

I was concerned about repercussions from this terrifying experience as I returned her to the foliage. I felt guilty about my intervention, but glad nonetheless. The next two days were not working days. Perhaps I would, after all, have the chance of being spectator and midwife at the lying-in.

It was not until Sunday, making it a full six weeks after mating, that, frantic at not finding her, I came upon her already scraping away on the surface of the sandy place she had chosen to dig.

In March the sun rises at about 4:30 A.M. and sets around 7 P.M. Midday is oppressively still and humid. Through the long hot day she dug.

A female's hands are not well-equipped for digging, so the whole operation is laboriously slow. The time taken depends on the type of earth and any obstacles or interruptions encountered. But the process takes at least twelve hours from start to finish, and sometimes much longer.

Topsy almost immediately came up against a large stone and, failing to dislodge it or successfully dig around it, started all over again. She dug at an angle; and as her hands loosened the sand and brought it up in armfuls under her body, her hind legs took over, collected it and pushed the small mounds backward, away from the entrance.

If, when her head was in the hole, the tremor of earth around her gave a warning of danger, she stopped digging, relying on this stillness to cloak her vulnerability. She slowly disappeared until only the end of her tail was visible. When the hole was about eight inches in length, she started trying it for size. Clearing all surplus sand from the entrance, she entered headfirst and tried to make a full turn inside so that her head looked out. If she could not do this in comfort, she backed out again and continued digging. The idea was to be almost invisible to the casual glance and thus be able to face any danger head-on while she was laying the eggs.

In the early afternoon, true to the small fellow's foreboding because I had denied i-Tekwane a meal, the wind started, teasingly enough at first, to harry the trees; then, in increasingly bad temper, to blunder about amongst the dark clouds, bringing lightning and rain. My companion fled.

Topsy had a perpetual cake of mud on her snout. I was drenched. My camera was given the benefit of the only protection I had—an old hat. Fortunately, we were on a slope and the rivulets bypassed us to a certain extent. She had started digging at about 6 A.M. At 4 P.M. she showed herself satisfied with the repository for her eggs by making a few full turns in it. Ten hours of hard labor. For a moment she lay there, her body heaving with effort and the burden of eggs. Then she turned, backed into the hole and shifted around until she felt comfortable.

At this stage, I gently sliced away a side of the hole, the better to photograph her. Although accustomed to seeing me, she did not allow taking anything for granted. She stayed quite still, making no effort to move away. Satisfied that my interference would still enable her to lay the eggs deep in the earth and consumed with urgency, she hunched her head over her neck and started to lay. Her body heaved in spasms as each egg left her, shining with mucus. Each was about one centimeter in length, oval and soft-skinned yet firm. Sometimes they came in rapid succession, half a dozen at a time; with others, there was about five minutes between. After each ragged layer, she turned her body and, with her hands, covered the eggs with a thin film of sand. I could barely comprehend that her body had held forty-one eggs. No wonder she had had so little space for food! The laying took thirty-five minutes.

Pathetically exhausted and, by this time, half out of the hole, she just lay there, indifferent now that she had fulfilled her function. There was still much to be done to ensure the safety of the eggs, but at the moment she was past caring; at least some of the eggs would now stand a chance no matter what transpired. Could she not leave it at that?

A chameleon spends most of its time in trees and is ill at ease on the ground, where it descends only to find food and, in the case of the female, to lay. It merges into the arboreal background with its green body.

Before the sun sets, a chameleon makes for a high branch or protected twig, locks the segments of its hands and feet around it, and sleeps there until dawn. In the beam of a flashlight, sleeping chameleons assume a pale luminous glow and are easily picked out.

The ability to-change colors serves to camouflage and protect the chameleon in its natural environment—trees. However, its color is also governed by temperature, emotion, and light. When a hanging flower partially obscures its body (*top*), the shaded area will appear lighter than the area exposed to the bright sun. Note the lighter triangular area where the flower had rested (*bottom*).

A chameleon's tongue is longer than the chameleon itself. It rests crinkled in the mouth, and when it is needed, two strong side muscles propel it forward at lightning speed to its full length. At the end of the tongue, a bulb with a shallow, hollow tip traps the prey. The tongue then whips back into the mouth, taking the insect with it.

A chameleon does not lap or suck up water; it presses its tongue against leaves and twigs that are wet with rain or dew.

The chameleon's head is like a bony helmet. Its skin is finely granulated and cold to the touch. It has no teeth, but its jaws are serrated. On either side of the head are unique eyes, spherical turrets that can move independently of each other.

Above—At the back of the male's hind feet there is a small "thumb" of hardened skin, used during mating to stroke the female and keep her stimulated. Here, the "thumb" on the left hind foot can be seen above the branch.

Left—The tail is prehensile, and if it is injured in any way, it does not grow again.

A chameleon enjoys a meal of grasshopper.

During the hot, humid summer, chameleons shed their skin an average of once a month, sometimes more. The old skin lifts away from the body, then starts to fray. This chameleon's tail was probably accidentally cut off by sugarcane field workers. The lack of a tail noticeably upsets its balance and its capacity to aim unerringly at insect food.

Left to right—A male courts a female with his mating "dance." The female's skin develops small yellowish mating spots, but she signals her unreadiness by rearing and hissing and blowing out her brightly colored throat. The smaller, duller male pursues the female up a tree. Three males struggle to mate with the female; only the most determined succeeds.

Left to right—A female bulges with eggs. She spends a day or two digging a hole for her eggs, then proceeds to lay around forty eggs in about one-half hour. Half dead, she must still cover the eggs with sand. Ten months later, the eggs hatch and the babies push up through the sand, tail first, with snout and tail together.

Dwarf chameleons bear live young. The babies are ejected in sacs which disintegrate immediately. The independent newborns immediately crawl off for cover, snap up available food, and press their tiny tongues against leaves or a mother's snout for water.

But Nature allows no slipshod workmanship, no letting up. Webs broken have to be repaired, nests damaged have to be rebuilt, tunnels caved in have to be reshored. Something started has to be finished, with remorseless drive, regardless of insurmountable hazard and consuming weariness. Life itself may depend on it.

She was propelled by sheer will power and unconscious instinct throughout the next three hours until darkness. From the mound of sand collected at the entrance, she started to fill in the hole with her hands. Hopelessly inadequate for the task, she collected only small armfuls with each effort. Again, as in digging, she mostly gathered with hands and pushed in with feet. Every so often she tamped the earth down with her elbows. Eventually, as darkness fell, there was little sign of the hole, and I waited for her to move away. But she closed her eyes and curled up over the hole that hid her eggs.

The dawn was as golden as the one when we'd met, but I had no thought of its liquid loveliness as I hurried to the forest. She was already astir, and there was a wide circle of disturbed soil where she had been gathering more covering for a hole already covered. And still she scraped. By the time the sun had forged into the swamp, she no longer knew exactly where the egg hole was. Her movements were those of an automaton, and they gradually became slower and slower, her direction more confused. At last she crawled away, fatalistic, oblivious of threat, her mission completed. I have seldom before, or since, seen such total dedication as in that eighteen-hour cycle.

For the following few days she stayed on the same low branch, not attempting to protect herself or feed herself. Then I noticed that what I believed to be a disinterest in food was, in fact, an inability to hunt it. Added to her extreme weakness and emaciated appearance, on odd occasions when a fly or grasshopper settled on a nearby leaf, the end of her tongue appeared but never quite reached the presented food. It had neither muscle strength nor, it seemed, lubrication to propel it. Sometimes more of it showed, but there was no sinewy whiplash—the tip had no impact and it lolled back.

She seemed capable only of opening and shutting her mouth, as though stimulating saliva.

There is a theory that after laying, a female chameleon crawls away to die. This would mean, of course, that those chameleons that mated the first year would not be full-grown when they died, while those that did not mate for a couple of years would continue to grow and live. In fact, the longer they escaped mating, the longer they would live. The more I watched, the more I could understand the root of the theory. Each female, no matter what age, became drained after laying to the point of near-unconsciousness, prone to starvation and exposed to danger. I often came across the dried-up bodies of females. A few were large, but most of them were only one season old.

Concerned at their distress, I nudged small insects toward those chameleons I had observed laying and succeeded in persuading them to take the food at close quarters without the aid of their tongues. More important, though, was their need of water. Even if shy about accepting sustenance while I was nearby, they did not hesitate to wet their tongues against the leaves I sprayed with water. And they were better for it.

After four days, during which she had had nothing but water, Topsy struggled to her legs, her ribs showing clearly through her skin, and took a few small grasshoppers with her jaws. Quite still, we looked at each other, sharing a solitary instant that went beyond the limitations of our diametrically opposite lives.

My mind could only register simple, unquestioned homage. But who can say what strange and deep instincts moved in her thin, cold-blooded body, what unknown decisions were being thrust upon her—a desire for a quiet release from suffering or a sudden flaring of the will to live?

SIX

Winter Waiting

As winter, with its shorter hours, ousted summer, chameleons seemed to melt away. Most went into hibernation. I came across them curled up in the whorls of aloes or wild banana leaves, and between the thick bark separated from the trunks of dead trees. Some stayed in the same place but out of sight, lethargic, indifferent to food. Others moved about sluggishly, not traveling far. I could find no hard and fast rule except that they all went into a state of semi-retirement for the cold months between June and August.

This may be forced on them by a lack of food, for during this time grasshoppers and insects are noticeably fewer in the fields and verges. Most had gone to earth and would not reappear in numbers until spring.

So I filled my winter weekends in the distant Drakensberg mountains or at home, seeking out the lethal poacher snares of wire that strangled small buck in the bush. A favorite place for hanging them is at head-level in the track—a tunnel in the undergrowth—that leads down to the water.

The Umhlanga River flows slowly through the reeds, one bank backed by sugar cane; the other steep, wooded, overgrown. One Sunday morning I followed a track to where it ended just above the river bank. As I wondered at the unseasonal heavy rain that had made the water rise and rush in a torrent to the sea, my small companion shouted: "There! Your friend drowns!" Shocked, I followed his outstretched hand. A hefty piece of branch revolved slowly in the force of the water, and each time it went the full circle, I caught a glimpse of a now familiar outline clutching a twig. Without thought I slid down the steep, sandy bank and leaned out to catch the branch. I could not reach. Crashing and blundering along the bank, I kept pace, but the branch gained on me until, without further ado, I plunged in and spluttered to shore with my prize.

The chameleon was black with cold, its feet frozen in a viselike grip. It would not be tempted to fresh foliage; it made no move to escape. So I had to cut its twig adrift from the branch and carry it home that way. Only its eyes told me that it lived, and they watched me with that poignant mixture of mistrust and hope with which the wild regards all humans.

I had thought that the few winter months would be void of chameleons, but I found myself with half a dozen casualties or near-casualties. These I placed in a "sick bay," which I made from a stretch of wilderness—bushes, creepers and grass—that I surrounded with low sheets of glass, a means of gently persuading any wanderers to remain in safety. But for most of them it was quite unnecessary. They were more than content to stay there. They were far from active, in any event, and although I introduced temptations for hibernation, they chose their favorite branches and spent most of their time there.

Although they evinced little interest in food, I felt a responsibility to supplement any they might find in the grass and shrubs. I armed myself with a small fish net and a bottle with holes in the lid, and designated Sunday mornings as my grasshopper time, making the fire breaks in the cane fields—

strips of shortish lush grass—my hunting grounds. In no time at all I had an audience of little Indian and Zulu children, and it was not long before I persuaded that audience to help. At first it was a game, with small financial gifts of appreciation from me at the end. Then a small, self-appointed paymaster of about ten years of age started figuring out how much each bottle of grasshoppers was worth, taking into account the size of the catcher so that everyone was happy. Often in the bottle among the grasshoppers, grass and weeds, I found a surprise when I arrived home—a small Microsaura chameleon. The lack of insects in winter was overcome. Happily, this saved me many hours of searching and allowed my cluster of small helpers and me to go down the river to the sea where, through lack of transport, they seldom had the opportunity to go.

During this time I was often confronted with death, which always left me feeling desolate. A chameleon once ailing seldom recovers. The ones I came across were more than likely the females that had tried, unsuccessfully, to recover after laying. Some I took home, knowing the signs of death upon them: sunken eyes, a body blotched with pale yellow and blue-black markings, jaws and tongue unable to function. They were doomed, and they died with patient acceptance. I was distressed and angry at my inability to help.

I wanted to bring Topsy to the chameleon reserve, but I could not locate her. I was not concerned, knowing that I would recognize her immediately by the scar left by i-Tekwane's beak.

I surrounded her eggs with sheets of glass. Her babies would be on their own from the moment they hatched. No one could tell me when this would be. I would just have to wait and watch.

To a chameleon devoid of any maternal instinct, those eggs were meaningless. But that small enclosure deep in the bush was full of meaning for me and held the solution to a mystery. It represented the end of one story and the beginning of another.

My chameleons—slow-moving, strange, pathetic in their helplessness—pinned me in a microcosm where I became acutely aware that life itself, often pitifully short in the wild, is a hard-won gift; where the perfection of Nature was both near and distinct; and where trivial happenings set me ablaze with such triumphant discovery that it was difficult not to wake all I knew to tell them.

SEVEN

Summer Mating

While Topsy's eggs were waiting in the earth and she and I were waiting for the spring, the males of our chameleon world were waiting for the females' only mating period which fell during January and February.

In that second year a curious fact emerged. Almost all the chameleons I saw in the garden or bush were females. Males were a rarity. Was it just that the females, larger and bright green, were more noticeable, that needing more food and being less timid they were seen more often near and on the ground; or that the males, quicker and more agile, were able to escape detection and only threw caution to the wind when looking for a mate? My eyes and concentration were attuned to finding them, but I seldom did.

By this time I knew the whereabouts of approximately twenty chameleons in bush and garden. As December drew the year to a close, I became anxious that my females would not mate that season. Science will explain that animals find mates through a powerful sense of smell, but I have always been intrigued how small members of the wild ever manage to find each other.

I need not have worried about Nature's efficiency. Suddenly males appeared virtually out of thin air. At first, they were resigned to crouching on bushes some distance from the females, who made it ominously clear that they had arrived too soon and would be unwise to rush their fences.

I watched the chameleon mating ritual countless times. In the beginning, I was unaware—besides the obvious overtures and threats—of the meaningful nuances, the imperceptible signs that passed between them or the final message of capitulation on the female's part that made the male, with a mixture of dignity and eagerness, approach her and know acceptance.

In Nature the wooing and winning of a female is an elaborate ceremony. At the crucial time, there is a great deal of aggression among the males because the field is competitive and all are determined to find a mate. Display is the only way for the male to advertise what a fine fellow he is and, with a lightning about-face, leave a challenger in no doubt of his hostile intentions should he try to interfere.

Birds are marvelously blessed with the wherewithal for successful courting. Males are endowed with bright colors, or they indulge in intricate dancing and aerial pageants, which they invite the female to share. There is head-shaking, bowing, rhythmical sequences full of the language of courtship. Penguins offer their mates stones as a pledge; some finches give twigs or grass. It's a colorful, fascinating way of projecting an image, more eloquent than any language.

A male chameleon is singularly at a disadvantage in the suitor game. He has little with which to attract a female, and he is, besides, smaller than she is, so he does not relish arousing her wrath. All he can do is wait patiently, guard the territory surrounding her and try by various ways and means to make her look at him. In the wild, as with humans, each animal has its own particular makeup, and courtship depends on the two creatures concerned.

One evening the sun was beginning to set, with the splendor typical of Africa, when I turned to home. Darkness comes swiftly. The bees in the wild morning glories were muttering urgent warnings to themselves to be gone, yet still they procrastinated, as I did, in the late afternoon glow. Cicadas were tuning up in readiness for the wild cacophony that splits the summer nights. In complete contrast, fireflies moved silently among the first faint shadows in the forest. A nightjar called once, as if signing off the day.

But I had forgotten the moon, which drew my full attention to its spectacular rising from the sea. It took over the world. As I swished through the dewed track, I automatically went past a group of tall bushes where I knew two female chameleons slept.

Territorial rights exist among chameleons, although they are not rigidly enforced or defended. I have watched a chameleon climb slowly up a tree before becoming aware that the part it approached was already occupied. There was no argument. The intruder moved away from close proximity to the occupier, even if only to another part of the tree. It was a voluntary decision on most occasions, although to add weight to its rights, a large female would sometimes blow out her neck and sway in warning. However, once accustomed to each other's presence, they seemed quite compatible.

In my garden, two females once even formed an attachment and made for the same branch each night and slept curled up next to each other.

There were quite a few chameleons dispersed about the fringes of the swamp, but they seemed to meet by accident, astonished at doing so. Those in the garden, when they came across others, merely stopped, then went their respective ways.

It was only during the mating spell that the tranquillity was disrupted.

I found the two females I sought, asleep in the moonlit trees. There was a disarming innocence about the way they slept, as though profoundly aware of their absurd exposure to danger but fatalistic in their inability to avoid it. Hands and feet locked them to the tree, tails were neatly curled. Their eyes were tightly closed, heads resting along the branch. I felt, as always, a sense of relief at finding those I knew. I had just turned to go when the moon caught another luminous fragment on a lower branch. I went for a closer look and found a smaller chameleon. It was a male, and he had fallen asleep while hopefully watching his prospective mate.

The next morning I woke early and discovered that the chameleon trio had not moved.

The courted female kept her suitor waiting almost all day.

The male made the first move by tentatively advancing, his tail waving. The female watched intently, her skin covered in telltale light spots. Her crouched appearance spelled protest, and the male took notice of this clear message of discouragement by stopping immediately.

But he could not stay idle for long, so he rose, swayed from side to side and blew out his throat, his whole demeanor one of entreaty, of requesting attention. The female, too, began to sway, but hers was more in warning. At times her spots completely disappeared. The male, hissing, made one or two peculiar little mincing steps forward and, finding she did not actively object, speeded up his approach with every intention of being decisive and taking her by surprise. Too late he realized his mistake. She was at him with a formidable display of outrage and clamped her jaws on his forearm. He managed to wriggle free but, in doing so, dropped. His fall to the ground was broken only when he accidentally struck a branch, and feet and tail made simultaneous contact.

All hunter, he crawled toward her again, this time with studied deliberation in place of his erstwhile nonchalant zest. One look at her made him acknowledge, for the time being, a lesson learned. Time passed with long spans of inactivity. She was motionless except for her eyes; but his whole body, although outwardly the epitome of patience, twitched with suppressed restlessness. He made one or two half-hearted gestures of defiance but did not pursue them.

I have known of males having to wait two and even three days before being allowed to mate. As in this case, the female was not just prolonging the mating preamble; her rejection was a sign of not being ready for him.

Whether, knowing this, he waited for that right moment or whether it was her impressive strength and viciousness that kept him at bay is difficult to say. I think possibly the former. The waiting, for him, inflamed his impatience, but it also increased his determination so that, at the critical time, desperate decision and the female's nod of approval seemed to coincide.

At times he was so comically fed up that I imagined him coming to the conclusion that it was time to make *his* displeasure known, that the way to treat a temperamental female was with masterly aggression. He jerked up to all four legs and tried to look larger than life. Now he added a clicking movement with his head, and this, together with a gyrating body and loud hissing, was a laudable example of male muscle-flexing.

Inscrutable, swiveling, female eyes watched his every move.

Then, imperceptibly, the whole tenor of the relationship altered. He suddenly realized that he had moved forward, and while there was no visible encouragement, there was also no outright rebuttal. He climbed toward her, stopping as he reached her, as though for a moment overcome by her size.

Once on her back he clung to her around her body. She remained utterly still, an anchor for them both.

It was then that I discovered a vital, visible means of sex differentiation, apart from overall size and shape and a thickening at the base of the male's tail. On the male's hind legs, at the back of each foot and between the two segments, there is a small piece of hardened skin, light brown to white in color, like a tiny thumb. Once having seen them, I wondered how I could have previously missed them, since now they stuck out like the proverbial "sore thumb." The female chameleon does not have them.

With both arms and one leg holding firmly to the female's body, the male used one foot to keep the female stimulated. The two toes opened to allow the "thumb" to caress her, then closed as he drew his foot slightly away before returning to make contact again. Although the "thumb" is important in the mating, it is not the actual male sex organ, which is protected by being hidden inside of the body.

The first mating lasted twenty minutes. The female abruptly terminated it by pulling quickly away from him and disappearing into the foliage. He purposefully followed, and she lashed at him. Undaunted, he pursued her relentlessly; and to escape him, she often dropped to the ground and tried to hurry away to a bush. But he always found her, caught up with her and overpowered her. They mated four times.

There were only a few variations in the dozen courtships at which I was present. The main difference was time, both in courtship and the number of times the chameleons mated. In quite a few instances, another male mated with the female during the day following her first mating.

But there was one very different drama happening right next to me, which, absorbed to the exclusion of all except the pair in front of me, I nearly missed.

The second female, a few bushes and branches away, was also being courted and was in the last stages of acceptance. She and the male faced each other, he on a lower twig, two pinpoint eyes focused brightly on her; she with one eye on him and the other flickering around like a roving searchlight. It was this eye that picked up approaching danger. Until now she had tried every device to make herself look larger; now she pulled her head back over her neck and backed into the leaves.

The male did not look behind him but read the signs. In unconscious reflex he swung around, snapping his jaws as he did so. He did a complete turn and faced his problem head-on.

Two other males bore down on him, challenging him for his intended mate—she whom he had spent so long courting.

Now, besides trying to keep his eye on her, he had to fight

two duels to prevent either of the contenders from reaching her before he did.

Watching the previous chameleon mating drama, I had been in a bubble, solitary and remote, enchanted by the gentler moments, accepting of the inevitable crueler moments. That story now seemed dim and unreal against the naked malevolence of the three writhing bodies locked in a frenzied will to win. Flailing arms, legs and tails clung grimly and broke apart, hurtling bodies to the ground only to return, with desperate speed, back to the fray. Blinded by jealous rage, they seemed to lose sight of the prize for which they so furiously fought.

The prize, instead of taking this opportunity to escape, crouched, as still as I, hypnotized by clicking jaws and venomous hissing in the triangular competition that could result in only one winner.

The eventual mating was spectacular. In a split second the three males flung free of each other and fell to the ground. This time, instead of joining together in battle, they came to a simultaneous decision that was incredible to watch. They converged, from different directions, not on each other, but on the female, climbing and clinging in frenzied haste to reach her first.

The victor hung on to her grimly, ducked his snout under her arm and tried to hide his head from the slashing attacks of the maddened losers. When I had a chance to sort them out, I gave a satisfied nod. He was the original wooer.

Under impossible conditions he still managed to stroke her, although in disrupted determination rather than the regular gentleness of movement. I hoped that failure would make the two unsuccessful candidates look for new hunting grounds and leave the mated pair in peace. Instead, infuriated, they stopped their futile attempts to dislodge the champion and turned their attention to the female. There she was—there, yet unattainable. With renewed, frantic anger, one climbed on her head and attempted to mate there; the other had to be content with grasping whatever he could as he swarmed over all of them.

The dazed female made no move until the holocaust simmered down, but her eyes were tiny volcanoes erupting in a kaleidoscope of rapidly changing sensations.

Eventually the two routed males turned on each other and, tails twitching in angry frustration, went their separate ways. Even the remaining, triumphant one was bowed by the whole tearing episode and, after a half-hearted second mating, disappeared into the shadows.

Pity coursed through me. The female was marked with scratches and one eye was closing up. Forlorn yet still, she moved to a higher branch. There was no sign of the males, but she knew she would have to keep watch until darkness fell.

I took her home. She had had enough for one day. And there, in my garden, she laid her eggs six weeks later.

But my day, already overflowing with Nature's continuous surprises, was not over.

On a dead branch, spectral in the last light of day, stood Topsy. She was at bay, but her courtier's bold advance stopped short as she stretched to her full size and, for good measure, head down, took one or two intimidating steps toward him. It was obviously not the first time they had mated, but it was equally apparent that there was to be no more. He conceded without argument and with distinct alacrity.

My mind spun with the unrestrained ways of the wild, the prevalent hostility alongside the quiet harmony. Those that hunted by night already stole from shadow to shadow as the moon rose in the sky. Those that slept closed their eyes in fatalistic oblivion.

The little kingdom of the wild throbbed quietly, canopied by infinite stars. Somewhere up there, I thought, there is a southern constellation of sixteen stars called Chameleon. I found that satisfying.

EIGHT
Old Legend, New Life

Even in the early hours, the forest wilted in the midsummer heat. Life was listless, sabotaged into an economy of movement by the remorseless sun.

A ground hornbill, in-Singisi, boomed like a tolling bell, announcing the dawn. I wondered why it should be so near the coast, then I remembered the Zulu interpretation of the perpetual conversation between male and female and smiled at my thought: Perhaps the female, at least, was only here on a visit. "I am going; I am going; I am going home to my relations," she called in a tone-different voice; and, after a while, her mate answered, masculinely indifferent, "You can go; you can go; you can go home to your relations." Femininelike, she was disbelieving of his callous acceptance of her threat. But they lived happily ever after in continuous argument.

The hornbill, which looks rather like the black turkey, is closely associated by the Zulus with rain. Seeing a group of them in deliberation among themselves is a sure sign that they are summoning rain. In some tribes, so strong is the association that in a time of drought, a hornbill is caught and killed. Any ensuing rain is believed to be the heavens' weeping for the unfortunate bird.

By noon the sun was white-hot in a clear sky. The only small sign of the hornbills' rain was in the capricious breeze that occasionally caught at the treetops with restless hands. It could be innocent, but like the Zulus I knew it could also be the forerunner of the hornbills' storm. Now only grasshoppers and small insects whirred haphazardly from one baked patch of earth to another. And bush crickets chose this unlikely time to rub front wings together in endless, monotonous chirping. At times grasshoppers took over with that strange sound produced by the rows of small teeth on their hind legs as they strike the veins of the wings. Only the males can vent their feelings in this way; the females' role is to listen. This midday chorus rose to a feverish pitch before it was drowned by the cicadas with their night music.

I never relished catching insects and grasshoppers to transfer to my garden reserve. I always had a fleeting sensation of being a Roman pitting Christians against the lions. But needs must. I wanted to be sure that my little lions were not denied the abundant supply in the Little Bush that would enable them to eat their fill during the "fat" months.

Wherever I disturbed the grass, the insects rose in a cloud, shimmering in the haze with the same magnetism as a will-o'-the-wisp at night. There always seemed to be more insects just beyond where I stood. Coarse sedge reeds matted with creepers marked the beginning of the swampy ground as, further on, the tall waving reeds denoted where the water took over. When the distant river had no outlet, the water rose in the lagoon and spread to the swamp. I could see this day that the river must be rushing into the sea, draining the swamp. It was a day when one could, by jumping quickly from island to island in the swamp, have an exhilarating run just escaping the squelchy mud before it turned into sinking footholds.

I was just about to aim for one island when I was gripped by the awful feeling of paralysis, of trying to freeze movement in midair. There, stretched before me in the undergrowth, was about four feet of python—the tail end.

Dithering from clump to clump around it, I had the lightning thought that at some time I had probably run near or over its head. Or was the monster curled around, as they often lie, so that its head was near me now? Wherever I went I could easily encounter the rest of it. This was no creature with predictable place for head and tail.

I was unable to stand still; if I did, the swamp sucked at my feet. From this precarious position I glanced at the distance to solid earth. There stood the two small Zulus shouting: "Nkosazane, come quickly. There is something for you to see." I called out: "Is it the big snake's head?" They consulted together, then one sang out: "Oh, no! The one we see is as small as a locust."

Some locust! I thought. There was nothing to do but return in the vague direction from which I had come.

About halfway back I saw why the python had made no movement. I leaped over undergrowth and a coil of the huge snake lay distended in the obvious shape of a buck, horns or hooves clearly protesting against the inside of the skin.

"You came quickly," they approved as I sprawled next to them, unable to throw off the feeling that I was being watched. So would you, I thought, if you were running on python, but I forebore to say anything that would add to their already ingrained fears.

We walked in single file along the edge of the swamp until we came to a bank overgrown with bushes and saplings. "There," one pointed in triumph. "And there, too," indicated the other. "We have found two for you, and is it not true that this one looks just like a locust?" Indeed it did. In size and color. It was a female, *Microsaura pumila*, full-grown to its five centimeters—a perfect dwarf chameleon.

I laughed in pure release at what I had expected to see, at the enormity of the huge reptile lying back there in the swamp, and at this little member of the same family. The "other one" was a small male; and delighted, I took them home, where I could watch them in my garden. The female was soon heavy with young, and the babies were born three months later.

I had often come across Microsauras, usually on guava and mango trees, where the bark and lichen were perfect camouflage for their special coloring. They are never green, but either an all-over beige, a deep velvet brown with yellow-brown horizontal stripes, or a mottled dark-light brown. Their snouts are pointed and their heads run naturally into their bodies, without flaps. The male is smaller than the female and usually beige in color.

Being so tiny, they are not easy to locate, but I soon had quite a colony, especially when the little Indian children in the cane fields knew I was interested in them as well as the Flap-necks. There are wild guavas aplenty in the wooded valleys among the cane. And the Microsauras are easy to feed, as a basic diet of fruit flies suits them admirably. They were soon quite content, abandoning themselves to sun and indolence.

In the afternoon, wind rippled through the distant cane fields as the storm built, waiting to prove the hornbill legend. When I made for home, the forest was beginning to seethe and the surf was a roar. The sky was filled with white sails of the Armada running before the wind, pursued by a smaller fleet of rain-filled clouds that bumped and jostled each other. From it suddenly sprang a perfect rainbow. Quite incongruous, I thought. Now, what?

Here was the Queen's Arch. Named after the wattle saplings that form the foundation shape of their beehive huts, this splendid arch, the Zulus believe, holds up the dwelling of the Queen of Heaven. Some tribes believe that a rainbow's colors reflect those of a snake that lives in the clouds; others believe that the snake lives in an ant heap; and yet others say the rainbow is God's Bow and that its colors bring the evil of fire and burning. A rainbow is neither loved by the Zulus nor found to have any beauty. This is because it chases away rain.

Who would win? The hornbill who called the rain or the rainbow that put it to flight?

Legend was powerful enough to sustain both beliefs.

The first drops hissed on the sun-dried sand and threw up puffs of dust. The wind tossed objects across my path— leaves, twigs, even a small nest flew past.

Something landed at my feet. It was a tiny pregnant Microsaura. This, I thought, must be the year of the chameleon, and without further ado, I took her home with the others and settled them on one of the most sheltered bushes I could find. Had I known she was so near her time, I may have acted differently; but I was always anxious for the chameleons to live naturally.

By evening, while the wind still gusted, the rain had lost its initial fury and was now a steady drizzle. It would soon stop, since the rainbow had reappeared to chase it away. I kept returning to see how my small Microsaura fared in the wildly jerking branches of the leafy shrubs. On one such visit I saw that the pregnant female now clung with her hands and feet to the edges of a large leaf. Concerned and just about to move her to a safer position, fearing that a leaf was no place for her awkward bulk, I noticed her eject a tiny sac onto the leaf. As it touched the wet surface it burst.

I shook my head in disbelief. From the steadily arriving sacs emerged perfectly formed midget chameleons, reflexing straightaway to secure any foothold that would anchor them to their windswept birthplace, where survival seemed an impossibility. Once riveted with tiny, newly born limbs, they instinctively raised minute heads, opened tiny mouths and pressed even smaller tongues against the leaves. Their first act was as independent as their whole lives would be. They drank their fill, knowing the offer of water had been made and had to be taken; there was no knowing when thirst could be slaked again.

The next morning stole upon the world with no presage from legend.

Still glistening with rain and looking just like raindrops themselves, all eighteen miniatures were there, already moving about in search of food. I put down some overripe bananas in the grass; and by mid-morning, those that were not sunning themselves on the long strands, like a string of small black pearls, were down flicking unbelievably tiny but deadly efficient tongues at the fruit gnats.

I knew that there were no parental ties in the chameleon family, but I did not then know that dwarf chameleons cannibalize their young. One morning I counted the babies and found that two were missing. The predator could have been either lizard or bird, so I sat and watched from a distance. I noticed the adults projecting unerring tongues at flies, grasshoppers and insects. As soon as there was the slightest movement they turned toward it, focused eyes and ate whatever came up on the ends of their tongues. Even their own newborn progeny.

The little Microsauras were utter enchantment. They were more approachable than the larger Flap-necks and, within a short time, were quite unafraid. The pregnant females especially were a delight in their bulky serenity. Their camouflage was very effective; and this, together with the absence of long and arduous egg-laying, seemed to make them less anxious and danger-prone than the Flap-necks.

Scarcely noticeable in the tapestry of the wild, they were nonetheless an intrinsic part of its completeness, offering small flecks of rich brown and beige that give substance to vivid colors.

I started to worry about Topsy's eggs. Birth is usually connected with spring, but August and September had long since passed and there had been no sign of their hatching. I despaired of its ever happening. One reference gave the incubation period as six weeks; another referred to a "very long incubation period." No one seemed to know. My one hope was from a man whose knowledge I respected but whose forecast of "nine to ten months" left me dubious.

Six weeks passed into eight weeks. Six months passed. Determined not to disturb the eggs if they were still in the earth, I had, nonetheless, checked daily the glass enclosure with its protective thick-foliaged shrub and grass for a sign of small life. Eight months passed. The temptation to discover what had happened to the eggs was past enduring. Still I hesitated to take the chance that might perhaps kill the contents.

Then it was December, and the hatching of eggs laid the previous March seemed hardly possible. They were so important that year because they were the only chance I had of determining the incubation period. Subsequently, the sites of the eggs soon to be laid by at least half a dozen females who were due to mate in January or February could be marked and carefully watched. It just meant another year's long wait. Stubbornly, too, I wanted Topsy's eggs to be the voyage of discovery.

If the incubation period did prove to be in the neighborhood of ten months, it meant that everything happened to chameleons between December and March. During this time they mated and laid; and, sandwiched in between, the babies from the previous eggs, laid months ago, should be hatching.

All this proved to be the case.

One of the small Zulu "chameleon shepherds" moved diffidently from foot to foot. It was not worthy of my attention, he said, but still, there it was. He had noticed it only because the birds were trying to eat it.

It clung to a reed—small, perfect and terrified as birds attacked it. When I rescued it, I noticed another one similar in size nearby. The two boys located three more. I did not think they were newly born, but they were still very small. They were baby Flap-necks. This, then, must be the time for the eggs to hatch.

In my enclosure the earth was undisturbed, the grass free of baby chameleons. I kept closer watch, exhorting the "shepherds" to do the same. Even so, I might have missed the event, as one misses so many things, if I had not stopped to watch a stick insect.

This one's thin body exactly emulated the stem of a weed; its head was the same pink as the minute cluster of flowers;

and its legs had the appearance of spindly leaf stalks. I marveled at its adaptation, pondered the rarity of the males of the species and the resultant sexless mating that still allows the female to lay fertile eggs. Idly, I watched it merge perfectly into the background and rear at a praying mantis before moving off. The mantis raised its front legs with their long spines as it waited to trap a susceptible insect, then eat it alive.

Having accepted long ago that nothing would come of Topsy's eggs, I gave the earth only a cursory glance. There were many more interesting things above ground.

Did the earth move a little?

The praying mantis gesticulated in wild benediction just above, and I hoped it was not threatening the source of the movement, small and unconvincing, that I waited to be repeated. I was sure that *something* had moved, and the small patch of earth suddenly seemed as important as an Egyptian tomb. Would it reveal the answer for which I had waited so long?

A flake of crusted sand cracked as it was tilted up, then was still. Nearby another small volcano erupted.

A tiny bright-green snout cleaved the sand and two minute hands pushed forward. Then came the head dominated by its eyes. Before shaking free of the sand, the eyes swiveled around, questioning safety. It was right to do so. I noticed, for the first time, that there were others watching—lizards on the ground, birds in the trees—waiting for the chance to snatch this scrap of life pushing its way into the bush. Its hand scrabbled for a hold and it heaved its shoulders, then the remainder of its body, into full view. Still slimy with the mucus from the egg and caked with sand, it moved instinctively for cover.

I was stunned. It had been in the earth forty-six weeks.

Others emerged, and I carefully cleared away the sand to watch the eggs. Before the baby broke through there was considerable movement in the egg. In some cases, even after this inner activity, the egg became quite still for several hours. There was a time lapse of thirty-six hours between the first birth and the last. I believed one or two eggs to be infertile until they hatched on the third day after the first youngster had arrived.

The eggs, soft when laid, had become so distended that when the membrane split, it was almost a burst. Inside I caught a glimpse of the tail wrapped alongside the body and up around the head. In one egg, the tail protruded first and waved around as though searching for an anchor. If there was any disturbance or sound, the baby withdrew its head and stayed curled in the egg, remaining there until it sensed that the danger had passed.

I accounted for all the forty-one eggs I had watched Topsy lay so long ago. Seven hatched and lived; twelve had been destroyed, probably by ants or other underground insects, and the husks of the shells were dried up; nine had not even started to develop and were possibly infertile; ten were at various stages of growth, the baby fully formed but not alive—it looked as though the egg membrane may have been pierced in some way, as it had collapsed around the body; and three looked as though, in trying to reach the surface, they had been too weak to cope and had been choked by their long tongues, which hung out of the side of their mouths filled with sand. Ten eggs, therefore, had developed into live chameleons; but only seven out of forty-one saw the light of day. This average—17 percent—proved fairly consistent in subsequent observations. Sometimes it was as high as 20 percent, sometimes it dropped to 15 percent. The number of eggs that hatched did not seem very many, but Nature had provided an initially high number to allow for the losses that beset reproduction in the wild.

I noticed, during the following years, that a higher percentage of eggs hatched when the months of incubation— mostly winter—were dry. If there was more rain than usual and the earth stayed damp for long periods, a greater proportion of the eggs rotted. More babies appeared to survive, though, if the midsummer months of their birth had regular rain. Not only was it easier for them to push up through soft earth, but they also thrived in the humidity, and vigorous leaf growth afforded greater arboreal protection.

I kept track of six of the seven youngsters. What

happened to the seventh I do not know. They all looked alike, but to me, each was identifiable. And was it significant that the one that had come into the world tail first always slept upside down? At first they all kept together, not moving far from their birthplace except to go higher into the bushes. At night they made for the same branches and slept in two groups.

Food was plentiful, but quite often they were like small children; and overambitious, they went for food that was too large for them and then struggled to swallow it. They needed moisture more than did the adults; and whenever the opportunity arose from rain or dew, they pressed their tongues against the wet leaves. At the end of the first month, they all shed their skins. Within two months they had doubled in size.

They were all born within thirty-six hours of each other, but development differed. Judging by size, four seemed to be females and two males, although at this stage—and not until a long time later—was there any sign of the distinctive male "toe." The flap over the neck did not become noticeable until the fourth month.

A year after their birth, although not as large as their full-grown mother, they were mature enough to mate. The number of eggs laid by these yearlings is considerably fewer than in older chameleons, and their chance of survival is greater if they miss mating in the first year.

I am always overcome by birth in the wild. Remote, dangerous, unattended, the first gulp of life is no lease on safety nor on life itself. I was always moved with compassion by the knowledge that a chameleon's triumph in hauling its tiny form from the dark earth, after so long, could turn into sudden extinction.

NINE
Ambassadors Extraordinary

During those days, I never tired of the little world in which the chameleons and their small fellow-beings moved. My original interest had matured into deep affection.

Naturally I did not expect my family or friends to share these tangents of mine from ostensible solidarity into the realms of the unknown, or to understand my dedication to a little cold-blooded animal that seemed to return little of my generous devotion.

It was the chameleons themselves who proved ambassadors extraordinary. Essentially wild, they had an endearing capacity to wear their oddness with grace and to brush with mankind in solemn and silent dignity. With these admirable traits they "won friends and influenced people" far more than any attempt of mine to generate interest or offer explanation.

They were themselves.

People who had given them little thought started by

glancing incredulously at a freakish creature, feeling compelled to comment that it had no right to be in the twentieth century, and gradually, without realizing it, became converts. I caught them unawares, staring at a chameleon with puzzled looks, trying to capture a profound and timeless thought.

In some people, the initial casual looking turned into a sort of tangible loyalty. Sheila, who lived next door, never passed up an opportunity, no matter where she was, to amass a supply of flying ants or grasshoppers, despite the caustic doubt of her husband and family; or regardless of traffic, to save otherwise doomed or maimed chameleons from roaring wheels on the highways. One evening as we sat on my veranda enjoying a cold drink, a large female chameleon came strolling down the front path straight toward us. "It's Samantha!" Sheila cried in a mixture of awe and delight. I had thought this female, easily recognizable by scars and a missing hind toe, and who had been around the garden over four years, either lost or dead, for I had not seen her in the past month. But Sheila would hear nothing to the contrary. Samantha, with a few more battling medals, thin and starving, had returned to safety and food.

Elsa, another neighbor, was asked to report progress on pregnant females about to lay. Little did she ever think that she would be giving regular bulletins on when a female chameleon had descended to the ground to look for a place to dig. When Elsa found it impossible to keep unobserved watch, two friends, Kay and Allan, obliged.

In Durban, at my office, anxiously hoping that the event would wait until the weekend, I gave little thought to what must be running through Elsa's mind until one day, impatient that I had heard no news for a few hours, I telephoned her. With a trace of bemused incredulity that this was happening to *her*, she said drily, "Don't worry. Your chameleon is not down on the ground; she's up the tree, just like you."

On another occasion, a female inconsiderately started to dig in the early afternoon. "Of course you must go home to her," agreed my boss, I thought a trifle hurriedly, in response to my single-minded and earnest plea. He agreed in that pacifying tone reserved for total incomprehension.

Time with my chameleons was deeply satisfying. But their very makeup did not invite levity, and the atmosphere around them was one of remote gravity. Despite this, they were often the cause of humor, mostly at my expense. One night, during my usual walk when I ensured that all were present and unharmed, I ended up in the lane that was bounded on one side by our bougainvillaea hedge. Oblivious that I was being watched, I flashed my flashlight up and down the thick foliage. A fisherman, returning from the beach, raised his old hat and inquired with infinite courtesy, "Can I assist in finding what you've lost?" Not stopping in my search, I said absently, "I seem to be short of a couple of chameleons." With a quick, determined slap of the hat onto his head, he hurriedly gathered his things together and moved quickly away, remarking over his shoulder, "Yes, well, good-night. I'll have to be on my way."

On another occasion I was looking for grasshoppers on the front lawn. I was used to spectators from the nearby block of apartments. So intrigued were they with this mysterious occupation of mine that they had no compunction about training binoculars on me. But one visitor, consumed with insatiable curiosity, came firmly up to me and asked; "You eat them, yes?" pointing to the bottle in my hand. I did not think this so very outlandish. He was a Frenchman, and after all, I knew his countrymen eat frogs' legs, so I replied, "No, not I. But I have a dozen hungry chameleons at home." Or, rather, that is what I thought I said. But my French obviously has its limitations. He fled. And I found out later that I had told him I had twelve starving camel drivers (*chamelier* instead of *caméléon*) to feed. After that I noticed him watching me with great intensity, possibly in the hope of spying, one fine morning, the camels of my camel drivers grazing on my lawn.

Throughout the week I could be with the chameleons only in the early morning and in the evening; but weekends and holidays gave me hours of immense joy in a wild kingdom. I made no attempt to tame them, and I seldom handled them. They just became accustomed to my moving quietly in their sphere.

Uncannily, the chameleons sensed the presence of strangers and often declined to eat or moved behind leaves when they were near. Some remained incurably shy and wary; others made me their willing slave, so outgoing that they lumbered to the ends of branches when I approached, their eyes flickering in constant hope of the possible grasshopper handouts I may have picked up on the way.

Often, when a female delayed laying for so long that her body was ungainly with eggs, I followed her journey from a distance as she climbed up and down trees, inspected the ground, wandered far and wide for her chosen place to deposit the beginnings of the next generation. Sometimes she took many hours; sometimes she ended that day's search by returning to the tree from which she had started out.

So that I could accurately record the gestation period, I kept, at one time, six females besides Topsy under close observation from the time they mated until they laid; then later, when I thought it nearer the time for the eggs to hatch, I surrounded the small area with glass and made sure that there was a shrub or large tuft of grass as immediate sanctuary for the hatchlings.

My journal records:

Samantha: Mated January 2, laid February 20 (7 weeks, 36 eggs). Hatched December 21 (44 weeks)

Rebecca: Mated January 26, laid March 15 (7 weeks, 38 eggs). Hatched January 5 (42 weeks)

Topsy: Mated January 31, laid March 13 (6 weeks, 41 eggs). Hatched December 18 (46 weeks)

Rose: Mated February 1, laid March 1 (5 weeks, 46 eggs). Hatched December 27 (43 weeks)

Dinny: Mated February 2, laid March 8 (5 weeks, 39 eggs). Hatched December 19 (45 weeks)

Abby: Mated February 9, laid March 22 (6 weeks, 39 eggs). Hatched January 24 (44 weeks)

Em: Mated February 9, laid March 10 (5 weeks, 40 eggs). Hatched January 26 (46 weeks)

Those females that went on living grew very large—larger than the average—and the longest life span among those in my orbit was at least five years. I may still come across that one again in my garden. She became even more like a prehistoric remnant with her older leathery skin and pronounced flap.

Besides having been lucky enough to fit the pieces of the chameleon mosaic together, I also experienced a wealth of exhilarating moments: observing the dedication that carries a female through the prolonged, demanding process of propagating her species; the birth of the dwarfs during a lashing gale; the constant appeal of a creature that can, paradoxically, be grotesque yet ineffably beautiful of line at the same time; and the harshly lovely world that surrounded the chameleons.

They were ambassadors to me, too, accepting me into their country, filled with unknown delights. Even when they did little but bask in the sun, I had time to let my eyes enjoy. Then I transferred my interest for a time to the minute marvels that, if I remained quite still, performed small miracles all around me—sexton beetles, undertakers of the wild, solemnly buried last night's dead; the arch-camouflagers displayed their talents, stretching the limits of detection to capacity; Nature's mimics studiedly resembled those insects avoided because of unpleasent smell or sting; ubiquitous ants hurried on their industrious way, stopping to communicate by rubbing antennae with fellow ants, while some of them milked the greenfly swarming up the stem of a flower. And, beneath the calm surface of the water where tiny boatmen and skaters skimmed, flashes of frail beauty stalked one another in the guise of magnetic color and innocent loveliness.

TEN

Salute the Little Lions

"Your heart cries," the old Zulu said quietly. I nodded. "And it is not for Umwabe that you grieve, Nkosazane. It is for yourself."

My head shook in quick denial, but he went on. "Umwabe will always look after himself. He is slow but wise. He will move away, and it will not catch up with him. Not since time began has it done so."

How had he divined my despair that "it" in the shape of time and progress was already beginning to encroach on my Little Bush?

I see the concrete of a giant building development rising above the trees, the bulldozed earth cascading over bullrushes that once swayed with the colorful bodies of weavers, bishop birds and their nests; over saplings and bushes where chameleons basked. I see the overgrown buck track machine-widened, trees pushed aside by mighty power. I can *see* the silence of the vacuum left by the fleeing wild, since it has the shape and form of menace.

I am silent, knowing the futility to stop it, knowing the old man is right: that I grieve, and that in this, the sixth year with the chameleons, they are moving away from the tide of man, that those content in my garden, now flanked by towering bricks, must soon be taken to join those seeking a new, distant place of peace.

I am silent, knowing that the tapestry we have woven will be rent with their going. I am glad that I was given time, patience and opportunity to see beyond the awkward surface. For there I found a gallant and admirable little creature abounding in distinctive attributes, with a headstart in time that commands respect and a disarming willingness to believe in me.

I could not help but feel a curious, incomprehensible aura of eternity about them as though chameleons had traveled down through time—serene, remote, unchanged; and that, with all my delving and proximity, my drawing them into the present, they would always be just beyond reach, mantled with the past.

The winter drew hoods around its days and the chameleons, lovers of the warm sun, knew it was time to move, both to somewhere against the cold and away from the raucous sound of man.

From the forest pulsed the sober song of farewell to my friend, the old Zulu lady, who had gone to join the spirits in heaven country. The chant alternately spoke of soaring release and agonizing loss, then crescendoed in glad belief that the ghosts of people live as long as they are remembered.

I sat listening, watching the chameleons I had brought to the swamp as a stepping stone for their next retreat.

Saturated in strange comfort, I borrowed that belief. The chameleons would be remembered; there were many people who would think of the little lions. I especially would remember: the infinite reward of knowing them; of seeing a way of life that is sieved through ceaseless endeavor, unwavering patience, quiet acceptance and constant danger.

I looked at two of these small lesser beings I had known

for a long time and hoped that their slowness in leaving was an echo of my reluctance to see them go. There was an empty splendor in the twin chameleon outlines gradually being silhouetted by the dying day. Tomorrow they would be gone.

In the expansive context of the wild, the two small creatures were quite insignificant. But in the isolation of the world we had shared, they were the radiant, vital focal point that had sparked my flight of wonder. I knew I would come looking for them; I should not be able to help it.

I watched them go. They faced their tomorrow, slow, defenseless, but with the inimitable courage and endurance of the wild. And they looked unforgettable, moving in their ancient mystery and unique reality.